City of LONDON
PAST & PRESENT

A pictorial record of the City of London

J.K. FISHER

© 1976 Oxford Illustrated Press and J. K. Fisher.

Set in 9/10 pt English 49 by Parchment (Oxford) Ltd.

Film, printing and binding by Chapel River Press, Andover, Hants.

SBN 902280 34 1

Oxford Illustrated Press Ltd., Shelley Close, Headington, Oxford.

Introduction

Extending from Tower Hill to Temple Bar and from the Barbican to the Thames, the City of London comprises only a small part of the London we know today — 677 acres, or just over one square mile to be precise. But the City performs very important functions, for although it has few residents and little manufacturing industry it is the financial heart of the nation, busily engaged in providing our 'invisible exports'. At the end of Queen Victoria's reign, when many of the old photographs in this book were taken, it was the nerve centre of the world.

In common with so many urban areas, the City of London has changed almost beyond recognition during the past century, and the following photographs indicate the nature and extent of the amazing transformation that has taken place. Yet throughout its long history the City has constantly been changing, and on a number of occasions the changes have been drastic and unexpected.

For example, over the years there have been marked fluctuations in the population of the Square Mile. In Roman times London grew very rapidly; it soon became the most important town in Britain and one of the largest urban centres in the western Empire. The city wall, which was constructed around A.D. 200, enclosed an area that extended from Ludgate to Aldgate and from Bishopsgate to the river, and by the late Roman period London's population may well have been around 50,000 — a figure that was probably not reached again until the fifteenth century. But when the Romans departed, London's prosperity suddenly declined and for a while the town may have virtually ceased to exist.

Recovery was very slow, and population growth was not aided by the high rate of mortality that prevailed in the dirty, disease-ridden city. From medieval to Stuart times plague was a constant threat: nearly two-thirds of the population died as a result of the Black Death in 1348, and about 20,000 perished in the Plague of 1665. Nevertheless, London continued to grow because trade was expanding and there was considerable immigration into the capital both from the provinces and from abroad. After 1665 the plagues receded, and the City's residential population remained relatively stable at a saturation level of about 125,000.

By now London was expanding rapidly beyond the city walls, and the well-to-do merchants and bankers were looking for places to live in the new western suburbs, away from the overcrowded and unhealthy conditions in the Square Mile, which was then the most densely populated part of Britain. This process gathered momentum in the nineteenth century when the improvements in public transport enabled many more persons to live in areas far removed from their place of work. Consequently in the mid-nineteenth century the residential population of the City began to fall, and the 'commuting age' began in earnest. At the end of the Second World War the number of City dwellers had dropped to a mere five thousand, and in Cripplegate, where the population density in Victorian times had been 350 to the acre, literally only a few dozen folk remained. This downward trend has recently been arrested by the Barbican redevelopment, but it is

highly unlikely that a large residential population will ever re-establish itself in the heart of the capital — the land is simply too valuable for that. However, the City is still very much alive during the day, and every morning from Monday to Friday a tidal wave of almost half a million people surges out of the main line stations, across the bridges and through the 'tubes', quickly filling up many hundreds of offices.

Changes have also been apparent in the functions performed within the City, although its importance as a centre of commerce has rarely been in doubt; Tacitus for example was able to describe Londinium as 'a busy emporium for trade and traders'. By the Middle Ages the City had developed a wide range of manufactures and all kinds of goods were being conveyed along the Thames. Woollen cloth was then the chief export, and the names of the various craft and merchant guilds — Skinners, Fletchers, Wax Chandlers etc. — bear witness to the surprising diversity of commercial activities being carried on within the Square Mile. Many of these trades are relatively unimportant today, while others have moved away from the City; for example after 1700 the craft of watch and clock making migrated north to Clerkenwell, where rents were lower. New functions like banking and insurance have since developed in their place, and printing, which first appeared in the late fifteenth century, has given rise to the great newspaper industry around Fleet Street.

The river front used to be a more or less continuous line of wharves, and ships moved constantly to and fro. Occasionally the river became so blocked up that vessels had difficulty in moving at all! By 1800 the volume of trade had increased so much that new docks had to be constructed downstream, on and around the Isle of Dogs. The river is therefore no longer the focal point of City life, although London is still one of the world's major ports.

It was in the Middle Ages that banking and money-lending first became important City functions, following the arrival of Jews from the Continent. The earliest type of insurance, marine insurance, was transacted by Lombard merchants in the fourteenth century. Not until after the Fire of 1666 was the first fire insurance company set up by a speculative builder called Nicholas Barbon, and it was only when the Empire grew and overseas trade expanded that most of the City's great financial institutions blossomed; Lloyd's and the Baltic Exchange started out in coffee houses in the seventeenth and eighteenth centuries respectively. Banks and insurance offices now seem to dominate the City at the expense of manufacturing industry and retailing, and during the past decade or so a great many foreign banks have established branches in the heart of London.

Nothing in the City has changed more during the past twenty-five years than its buildings. However, a closer look at the history of our capital reveals that there is nothing uncommon about redevelopment on such a massive scale. Roman London contained many fine and solid edifices — temples, baths, centrally-heated mansions, and a great basilica

— but they were all replaced in Saxon times by flimsier, wooden constructions that were easy prey to fire. London was sacked by the Danes in 851, and major fires, each of which destroyed a large part of the city, broke out at approximately one hundred year intervals up to the year 1212.

The Dissolution of the Monasteries changed the face of the City at a stroke. Many acres of land that had hitherto belonged to religious houses were soon put to new uses, and schools, taverns and tennis courts appeared where cloisters and chapels had once stood. Yet these changes were nothing compared with the devastation wrought by the Fire of 1666. 436 acres were laid waste in the conflagration which lasted for four days, and this included 13,000 dwellings and 88 churches. The new buildings may have been built to stricter standards, but as Smirke later observed, this did not prevent a vast quantity of bad bricks from being 'fraudulently made up with the old and half-decayed materials of the ruined city', and so the City virtually had to be rebuilt again in the second half of the nineteenth century, when the Victorians pulled down no less than four out of every five existing buildings in order to put up something bigger, more solid and more elaborate. Large areas of slums and many gloomy courts and alleys were replaced by purpose-built office blocks, and the City was at last worthy to be called 'The Heart of the Empire'.

Rebuilding continued at a furious pace right up to the beginning of the last war, when, as a result of the Blitz, one third of the City once more lay in ruins. Great towers of glass and concrete have now risen from the ashes, symbols of the confidence which is shown in the City as a centre of world trade. The new air-conditioned tower blocks may look plain and even ugly from the outside, but as places to work in they are surely preferable to the dark and somewhat stuffy nineteenth-century buildings. We can be thankful too that some of the best architecture of the past has been preserved and that some of the modern architecture is worthy to stand beside it — the new St. Paul's Choir School and the Central Criminal Court extension come instantly to mind.

Streets tend to suffer less in the cause of progress than buildings; indeed several of the most important traffic arteries in the City, like Bishopsgate and Ludgate Hill, have managed to survive for almost two thousand years. Yet if we compare the streets shown on a sixteenth-century map with those on the modern plan, the differences stand out more than the similarities. For instance most streets have undergone subtle changes in alignment, not all of which can be attributed to the shortcomings of the early map maker. Furthermore, many of the main thoroughfares in today's City were simply not there in Elizabethan or even Georgian times: Holborn Viaduct, Queen Victoria Street, King William Street, Byward Street — to name a few. Streets that were once main roads, like Fish Street Hill and Snow Hill, have now faded into insignificance. Others, such as Water Lane have disappeared completely, and one or two, like Jewin Crescent, have come and gone — dying in infancy.

With its two thousand year history, its ancient system of government and its love of pageantry, the City of London is often regarded as a stronghold of tradition. But the City also has a progressive spirit; it must function efficiently, and so its traditions have to be carried on within an environment which is constantly being adapted to meet changing circumstances. On past evidence, the City of the twenty-first century will be a very different place from the City of today.

J. K. FISHER

List of Illustrations

ACKNOWLEDGEMENTS

The author would like to thank Ralph Hyde, Keeper of Prints and Maps at Guildhall Library, for much helpful advice during the preparation of this book. The following have kindly permitted photographs to be reproduced:

The Commissioner of Police for the City of London: 12, 21, 22, 35 (Cross Collection); National Monuments Record: 9, 13, 16, 20, 24, 29, 40, 51; Aerofilms Ltd.: 28; Paul Popper Ltd.: 39; Archie Handford Ltd.: 29.

The modern photographs were all taken by the author except for no. 6, which is by M. D. Trace.

The old photographs were selected from the extensive collection at Guildhall Library.

1. TEMPLE BAR, 1877

When there is a Royal visit to the City, this is traditionally the place where the Lord Mayor meets the Sovereign and surrenders the City's pearl sword. Originally, Temple Bar was just a chain slung between posts, but this was later replaced by a timber building spanning the street. After the Fire, Wren designed a new Temple Bar which was completed in 1672. By the mid-19th century the structure had become unsafe and so it was dismantled in 1878. Although suggestions were made for re-erecting it in Temple Gardens or Epping Forest, it eventually ended up in Theobalds Park, Hertfordshire. The present memorial was unveiled in 1880.

Until 1772, Temple Bar was decorated with the heads of traitors. People used to gaze at these gruesome objects through spy-glasses which could be hired for ½d.

2. STAPLE INN, *c*1875

Staple Inn is a familiar landmark and a fascinating relic of old London. At one time it was a meeting place for wool merchants. In 1884 Staple Inn was sold to the Prudential Assurance Company who renovated the facade. The building dates from the reign of James I, and although much restored, it is a fine example of early 17th-century 'street architecture'.

Opposite Staple Inn is the site of Holborn Bars, where tolls were once levied on the vehicles of non-freemen entering the City. In the 15th century the road here was described as 'so deep and miry that many perils and hazards were thereby occasioned'. The state of the road has improved considerably since then, but the motor car still presents plenty of perils and hazards.

3. HOLBORN CIRCUS, c1890

Holborn takes its name from the 'Holeburne', or stream in the hollow, which once ran down the hill into the Fleet River. It is not certain whether the stream existed in historical times. The circus was constructed in 1872, shortly after the completion of Holborn Viaduct, and the bronze statue of the Prince Consort was added two years later.

At the turn of the century, this corner of the City had a pleasing architectural unity which unfortunately has since been destroyed. However, buildings which were hitherto concealed have now been exposed, and St. Andrew's Church, the largest of Wren's parish churches, is clearly visible on the right of the modern photo, as is the City Temple in the centre. St. Andrew's once served one of the most extensive parishes in London. In 1941 the interior was burnt out in an air raid, but it was restored and reconsecrated in 1961, and the exterior has now been cleaned.

4. HOLBORN VIADUCT, west, 1869

The date is 8 July 1869. Two foremen stand proudly on the new Holborn Viaduct — one of the triumphs of mid-Victorian engineering. A viaduct had been talked about for over a century; indeed, it was an obvious improvement for the steep inclines on either side of the Fleet Valley were a great hazard to traffic. Work was eventually commenced in 1863, and the 1400 foot long bridge was opened by Queen Victoria on 6 November 1869. Shortly afterwards there was considerable alarm when cracks appeared in the granite supporting piers, but so far the Viaduct has not collapsed. Besides benefitting traffic, the project involved the clearance of a large slum area, and over four thousand dwellings were demolished.

The original north-west Step Building has now been replaced, and at the moment there is a large gap in the distance where Gamage's store previously stood.

5. FARRINGDON STREET, 1869

This early photograph shows the south side of
the Holborn Viaduct eight months before
completion. Beneath the Viaduct runs
Farringdon Street, following the former
course of the River Fleet.

Several centuries ago the Fleet was so broad
and deep that ships could sail up it as far as
Holborn Bridge, which stood on the site
depicted here. However, the river was
encroached upon, and it degenerated into an
open sewer — 'very stinking and noisome' —
and notorious for the number of dead dogs
that it carried out into the Thames at
Blackfriars. The 'Ditch' was converted into a
canal, forty feet wide, in 1670, but this did not
prove a success and it was covered up in 1733.
A market was built on top of it. Later, the
market was removed and Farringdon Street
took its place. The river still runs beneath the
road — in pipes.

6. SHOE LANE, 1871

The construction of the Holborn Viaduct and the new Blackfriars Bridge necessitated better communications between the two. So in 1871 St. Andrew's Street and St. Bride's Street were driven through a maze of dark old alleys, linking the new circuses at Ludgate and Holborn. This view, looking south at the junction of Shoe Lane and St. Bride's Street (on the left), shows construction well under way, though everyone has readily downed tools in order to experience the novelty of being photographed.

In those days Shoe Lane contained an astonishing variety of small trades such as quill merchants, emery powder manufacturers, oilmen and leathersellers. They have now been superseded by more familiar activities such as publishing. The corner shown here is at present occupied by the Daily Express building, and dominated by the massive, seventeen-storey International Press Centre.

7. NEWGATE PRISON, *c*1890

The 'New Gate' once stood on the extreme left-hand side of this photograph, straddling Newgate Street. It was used as a prison for debtors and felons from the 12th century. The prison shown here was begun in 1770. Five of the Cato Street conspirators were executed outside its walls in 1820, following the discovery of their plot to murder the Cabinet Ministers at a dinner in Grosvenor Square, and a postman suffered the same fate in 1832 for stealing a letter. In 1807, when 80,000 people turned out to watch the hanging of Messrs. Haggerty and Holloway, twenty-eight of the crowd were trampled to death and seventy-five were injured.

The gaol was pulled down in 1902 and the Central Criminal Court was erected in its place. The northern part of Old Bailey, the street leading off to the right, is clearly separated into two lanes; the island in between was once occupied by houses.

8. HOLBORN VIADUCT, east, *c*1890

All the essential ingredients of a typical late Victorian street scene are displayed here: the policeman on traffic duty, the ornate gas lamp, the gentleman carrying a can of milk, and the rickety 'knifeboard' omnibus, full of top-hatted stockbrokers. The turning on the right in the middle distance is Snow Hill. It is difficult to imagine that this was once the main road across the Fleet Valley, just as it seems almost unbelievable that as late as 1864 people were paying considerable sums of money for a grandstand view of 'the drop' outside Newgate Gaol, which was situated just behind the camera.

The church of St. Sepulchre — now overlooked by Remington House and partly hidden by trees — dates back to the 12th century. It was rebuilt in the 15th century, repaired by Wren after the Fire, and restored by the Victorians in 1878. The church contains a musicians' memorial chapel.

9. SMITHFIELD, 1905

Once the 'Smoothfield', Smithfield later became famous for its fairs and tournaments. For many centuries a great open-air horse and cattle market was held here, and nearby streets were full of slaughter houses; Dickens described the ground on market morning as being 'nearly ankle-deep with filth and mire'. However, the processions of sheep and cattle through the city streets were a menace to pedestrians and traffic, and the danger to public health persuaded the Corporation to remove the live-meat market to Islington in 1855. The dead-meat market, shown here, was built on the north side of Smithfield in 1868. It is the largest market of its kind in the world, handling around 300,000 tons of produce each year. A large underground car and lorry park was opened in 1970, but the exterior of Horace Jones' building has remained substantially unchanged.

10. CHARTERHOUSE STREET, c1890

Here the camera is pointing eastwards along Charterhouse Street from the corner of Farringdon Road. On the right can be seen the Meat Market (which figured in No. 9) and the Poultry Market. The latter was badly damaged by fire in 1958, and a new building was completed in 1963. Charterhouse Street dates back only to 1869. Previously the main line of communication had been north-south, *across* the site of the Central Markets, between West Smithfield and St. John Street. Early maps show this route as the main road between the village of Islington and the City.

In 1890 the shops in the foreground were definitely the place to come if you wanted to buy clothes; there was 'a scientific cutter in attendance' at the tailor's on the corner, and further down the street you could purchase 'specialité trousers' at the attractive price of 10s 6d.

11. CLOTH FAIR, 1913

Cloth Fair is one area in the City which still retains a little of the 'olde worlde' atmosphere — that is as long as one turns a blind eye to the parking meters, the motor car and Lauderdale Tower in the background. It is also worth noting that the antique-looking kerb posts were not there in 1913.

The derivation of the street name is obvious, but who would believe, looking at such a narrow and insignificant street, that until Elizabethan times it was the site of the greatest cloth fair in England? The street was still inhabited by clothiers and tailors in the early part of the Victorian age, but when this photograph was taken it was chiefly geared to the nearby Smithfield meat market.

Since then most of the very old houses in this street have been removed, and the kink in the road appears to have been ironed out slightly.

12. ALDERSGATE STREET, 1944

On 13 June 1944, after preliminary trials, Hitler began to launch his flying bombs against southern England and against London in particular. The first bomb fell on the City five days later. With a range of 150 miles and a ton of explosives on board, the V-1s were capable of causing extensive damage as this photograph, taken at the corner of Long Lane looking north, clearly shows.

Two centuries ago this stretch of road was known as Pickaxe Street, and both sides were lined with coaching inns. In the foreground on the left was the Cock Inn (now the site of the Barbican station), and opposite was the Cross Keys Inn (now the site of John Trundle Court — part of the Barbican development). It was at inns such as these that travellers spent the night before setting out on the long journey to the North.

13. ST. MARTIN'S LE GRAND, c1900

St. Martin's le Grand really was grand in 1900, for then it was dominated by the magnificent Post Office, designed by Sir Robert Smirke. This building was erected in 1824-9 on a site that had been occupied centuries before by a collegiate church with special rights of sanctuary. The area had harboured many villains, and criminals sometimes made a last desperate attempt to escape here on their way to the scaffold at Tower Hill.

Smirke's Post Office was pulled down in 1913, and the present buildings — perhaps not quite so distinguished — were put up between the wars. The street has now lost much of its former character; only the building on the far corner of Gresham Street is recognizable in both photographs. The three triangular Barbican towers, one of which can be seen in the background, are in fact the tallest residential buildings in Europe.

14. BLACKFRIARS BRIDGE, 1903

The first Blackfriars Bridge was begun in
1760. It was originally going to be called Pitt
Bridge, after William Pitt, Earl of Chatham.
A toll of ½d was exacted from every person
crossing over it, and this was increased to 1d
on Sundays. Such exhorbitant charges led to
rioting, and in 1785 the tolls were removed.
The foundations of the original bridge could
not cope with the increased scour of the river
when old London Bridge was removed, so a
new one was built; it was completed in 1869
and widened in 1907-8. In 1967 improvements
were made to the northern approaches, shown
here, and east-west traffic now speeds
beneath New Bridge Street along electrically
warmed roads.

Notice the solitary motor car on the right,
attempting to edge its way through a crowd of
hansom cabs and omnibuses.

15. VICTORIA EMBANKMENT, c1890

A Thames embankment had been envisaged by Wren in his plan for rebuilding London after the Fire, and further elaborate schemes were drawn up by Colonel Trench and John Martin (the painter) in the early 19th century, but it was not until 1870 that the embankment became a reality. Over thirty acres were reclaimed from the river, and many old wharves had to make way for the great granite wall and the hundred-foot wide road behind it.

Dominating the old photograph (taken from Blackfriars Bridge) is De Keyser's Royal Hotel, opened in 1873 and replaced in 1931 by the unmistakable Unilever House. The Royal Hotel was founded by Sir Polydore de Keyser, the first Roman Catholic since the Reformation to become Lord Mayor of London. The District Railway Station, built in 1870, now looks rather forlorn, having been divested of its oriental onion tops.

16. NEW BRIDGE STREET, 1904

This photograph was taken from the balcony of the Royal Hotel, looking east. The Hand in Hand Insurance building was erected in the late 19th century on a site which had previously been occupied by a hospital for skin diseases. Now it has had to make way for road improvements, but the Black Friar public house is still visible behind. This busy junction has now become so dangerous for pedestrians that subways have had to be constructed. Spiers and Pond's Stores and the old Times buildings have been replaced by new offices which have not been allowed to obscure the dome of St. Paul's. Blackfriars Station was originally on the south bank of the river, but it was later moved to the north bank, and it is currently being rebuilt — as is the railway bridge across the street. Ludgate Hill Station (behind the Hand in Hand building) has now been closed.

17. QUEEN VICTORIA STREET, c1890

Queen Victoria Street had been in existence
for a bare twenty years when this photograph
was taken. It was certainly not a one-way
street in 1890, although the photograph gives
the impression that it was. Presumably the
Victorians had little sense of lane discipline!
The Victorian office blocks have now almost
completely vanished, although the British and
Foreign Bible Society building is still there in
the middle distance on the left, dwarfed since
1933 by the Faraday Building. The Times
Newspaper Office in the foreground has also
gone, and the site has been taken over by the
Observer.

On the south side of the street there has
been wholesale demolition to make way for
the North Bank Development, where a new
City of London School will be built. From the
time of William the Conqueror to the Great
Fire, this area was occupied by Baynard's
Castle.

18. LUDGATE CIRCUS, 1873

Here we see the corner of Fleet Street and
New Bridge Street as it existed in July 1873,
prior to the completion of Ludgate Circus in
1875. This south-west corner was the last part
to be demolished; the buildings were
presumably about to be vacated when the
photo was taken, as the outfitter is holding a
closing down sale. St. Bride's Church, where
Samuel Pepys was baptised, can be seen in the
top right-hand corner.

This junction was once the site of the Fleet
Bridge, which Stow described as 'of stone, fair
coped on either side with iron pikes'. Persons
bringing corn into the City had to pay tolls
before crossing the bridge, and ships coming
up the River Fleet often unloaded their
merchandise here.

Before 1860, when the Victorians began to
reconstruct large parts of the City, most of the
buildings in the Square Mile were similar to
those depicted in the old photograph.

19. LUDGATE HILL, 1902

Ludgate Hill has frequently attracted
controversy. The statue of Queen Anne
outside St. Paul's has been criticised ever
since it was erected in 1712; Malcolm records
that 'the wits of the day were very severe upon
it and on the manner in which the Queen is
placed, with her back to the Church and face
to the brandy-shop', and at various times the
poor Queen has had her sceptre, globe, arms
and nose broken off. The present statue is a
replica of the original, erected in 1886.

In the distance is the Ludgate Viaduct,
which for many years has spoiled the view of
St. Paul's from Fleet Street. Like Juxon House
on the right (which predictably caused an
outcry when it was built in 1964), it now seems
to have become an accepted part of the
scenery.

20. ST. PAUL'S CHURCHYARD, 1905

The present St. Paul's Cathedral — Wren's masterpiece — was completed in 1710 and has since become the most famous landmark in England. The Churchyard is much older for it encircled the medieval cathedral; the south side of it is known as 'the bow' and the north side is known as 'the string' on account of their relative widths. The narrower 'string', which is depicted here, is at present reserved for pedestrians, although even in 1905 through traffic generally used the southern route.

Several of Shakespeare's works were first published here, and the Churchyard was inhabited by booksellers right up to the last war. The only pre-war building to survive on the north side of the Churchyard has been Wren's beautiful Chapter House, which can be seen on the left. Note that everyone in the old photograph is wearing a hat; no self-respecting Edwardian would have been seen in the streets without one.

21. PATERNOSTER ROW, c1945

This is all that was left of Paternoster Row and its immediate neighbourhood after the Blitz. Gone are the densely packed Victorian shops and offices, and the once dark and narrow streets have become mere outlines; Paternoster Row runs along the bottom of the photograph and Paternoster Square — once the site of Newgate Market — can just be seen above the circular water dams.

Christ Church, on the right, is still in ruins, but otherwise the area has been completely rejuvenated. Shops, restaurants, pubs and cafés have been arranged around a series of 'linked spaces'; the squares have been raised above the old street level, and pedestrians are now segregated from vehicles, which are parked underground. The area used to be an important centre of the publishing trade, but much of the office space is now occupied by the Central Electricity Generating Board.

22. WATLING STREET, *c*1945

The previous photograph showed the bomb damage to the north of St. Paul's. Here we see the devastation on the eastern side. The cathedral itself certainly had a miraculous escape. Watling Street runs down the centre of the photograph, parallel to Cannon Street on the right, and Friday Street runs at right angles to these two roads, in the foreground. The distinctive tower of St. Mary Aldermary stands out in the centre, though it is rather less conspicuous today, hemmed in by great walls of concrete and glass.

The present skyline is very different from the one that existed in 1945, and it bears no comparison to the skyline of three centuries ago, which artists depicted as a forest of steeples rising above low, pointed rooftops. In the modern City the rooftops are much higher and flatter. Many of the ancient churches have been destroyed, and those that remain have mostly been outgrown by the post-war forest of tower blocks.

23. CHEAPSIDE, west, 1899

The Pioneer Quilting Co., the Great Western Railway Office and the City Toy Shop were about to be pulled down when a photographer had the good sense to record them for posterity. A Victorian would have great difficulty in recognizing this spot today, for it is now presided over by the octagonal Bank of Boston House, erected in 1970. A small but attractive garden has been laid out in front and the sharp corner of Newgate Street (on the right) has been rounded off.

Paternoster Row leads off into the background on the left. It dates back at least to the 13th century, taking its name from the makers of prayer-beads who drew their custom from worshippers at nearby St. Paul's. Before the Fire of 1666 the nobility flocked to the 'Row' in their coaches in order to buy clothes, causing the street to become 'so stop'd up that there was no passage for Foot Passengers'.

24. CHEAPSIDE, north side, c1900

Few statues can have travelled as widely as that of Sir Robert Peel (also visible in No. 23). Made of bronze and weighing seven tons, it was erected by public subscription in 1855 to commemorate the founder of Britain's police force. It had to be removed from Cheapside in 1935 as it was obstructing traffic, and it has since resided in the Bank of England Printing Works, Postman's Park, and the Metropolitan Police Training School at Hendon.

Foster Lane is hidden in the old photograph, but the buildings on the corner have now been cleared away, revealing St. Vedast's Church. The omnibus on the left proudly flies the Union Jack and advertises a most unlikely-sounding route, namely 'North Pole — Wormwood Scrubs — London Bridge'. The North Pole was in fact a public house near the Scrubs; it was an appropriate name because in 1900 this area was on the outermost fringe of London.

25. FRIDAY STREET, 1908

There was a most extraordinary scene on this corner in October 1846 when the wood-block paving was being taken up in Cheapside. It had been announced that persons who so wished could remove blocks themselves and take them home for firewood. Not surprisingly, this led to a mad scramble, and several people were hurt in the ensuing scuffles.

Seventy years ago, Friday Street was lined with warehouses and wholesale businesses, though long before that it had been the site of a Friday fish market. The shop depicted here was the oldest building in Cheapside, having survived the Fire of 1666.

Friday Street sustained severe damage during the war, and the northern part of it is now just a footpath through the Bank of England extension, which covers the area between Bread Street and New Change.

26. BREAD STREET, 1895

The old photograph clearly shows the mirrors
that were provided to reflect light through
windows that faced onto dark, narrow streets.
They were once a common sight in the City,
but nowadays buildings tend to have larger
window areas and interior lighting has
improved greatly, so that mirrors are
unnecessary.

Once the site of a bread market in medieval
times, this street was later inhabited by many
wealthy merchants. John Milton was born
here in 1608 and was baptised in Allhallows
Church, which stood on the south-east corner
of Watling Street until 1877. The site was
marked by Milton's bust, which can be seen
embedded in the wall on the right of the old
photo.

Most of the buildings in this street were
bombed in the war, and the ruins can be seen
in photograph No. 22.

27. CANNON STREET, *c*1890

This is the point where Cannon Street crosses Queen Victoria Street. The camera is pointing eastwards along Cannon Street, a name which is a corruption of Candlewick Street, and which appears in a document of 1276 as Candelwykestrete. The western part of Cannon Street is a relatively new addition to the map, having been carved out in 1853–4 at a cost of £200,000. The fine building in the centre (erected in 1871) used to dominate the crossroads, but now it cowers beneath massive modern office blocks.

In comparing the two photographs, one is immediately struck by the numerous directions and commands and the prevailing sense of order in the modern scene: arrows on the road, arrows on signposts, white lines telling you to stop or keep in lane, no entry signs, traffic lights — how *did* the Victorians manage without them?

28. QUEEN VICTORIA STREET, east, 1897

Preparations for Diamond Jubilee Day are here almost complete. The excitement of the occasion is reflected in the flags, the man selling special large-scale maps of London (3d each), and the photographer recording the scene from the steps of the Mansion House. Notice especially the grandstands on the roof of the Royal Exchange. Is that an umbrella on the top deck of the bus or is it a parasol, shielding its owner from the midday sun?

There can be few people today who would risk walking down the middle of Queen Victoria Street with their backs to the oncoming traffic, and at present one is sensibly only allowed to cross the street at certain times and in certain places. We have come a long way from the days when the road belonged to the pedestrian!

29. CHEAPSIDE, looking east, 1931

Since Victorian times Cheapside has undergone two complete transformations — once at the turn of the century and again during the Second World War, when even the venerable church of St. Mary le Bow was practically flattened.

Cheapside has always been one of the City's most important shopping streets; 'cheap' is in fact an old word for market. In times past, bakers of bad bread were dragged along this street on a hurdle before being made to suffer an hour in the pillory. Every shop used to have a sign hanging outside which told passers-by what was being sold inside. These hanging signs were prohibited in 1762 because they were always creaking and groaning in high winds, and on occasions they fell down, injuring pedestrians.

Between the wars Cheapside displayed a remarkable variety of flamboyant facades, but these have now mostly been replaced by the more staid architecture of modern times.

30. GUILDHALL, c1890

Guildhall is the centre of the City's
government and civic life. It has been the
scene of the most lavish banquets as well as
several famous trials such as that of Lady Jane
Grey. We do not know the exact age of
Guildhall, but it has certainly occupied this
site at least since the 12th century. It has been
burnt down, rebuilt, modified and enlarged
many times so that of the medieval building
only the crypt and part of the walls remain.
The present south porch, the style of which
has been described as 'Hindoo Gothic', was
completed in 1789.

Guildhall was badly damaged by bombs in
1940, but it has since been restored to its
former glory. The old Justice Room (on the
left) has recently been demolished to make
way for an enlarged Guildhall Yard, and the
fine new west wing was completed in 1974.

31. CRIPPLEGATE, 1897

The damage depicted here was the result of the Cripplegate fire of 1897 — one of the worst the City had seen since 1666. 550 firemen and policemen were called to the blaze. Fanned by a south-west wind, the flames quickly spread towards St. Giles' Church, damaging the vicarage (in the foreground). The beautiful and historic church, where Milton lies buried and where Oliver Cromwell was married, had a narrow escape. Today it is almost the only pre-war building left in the area.

Although the fire destroyed a great many Victorian warehouses, they would certainly have disappeared in the Blitz, forty-three years later. Now the imaginative Barbican Development is nearing completion. This will provide an Arts Centre and over two thousand flats (linked by means of elevated walkways) set among eight acres of landscaped gardens and lakes.

32. LONDON WALL, looking west, 1958

The street known as London Wall once ran along the inside of the city wall between Old Broad Street and Cripplegate. The route continued to the east as Wormwood Street and Camomile Street, both named after wild plants which grew out of the cracks in the crumbling defences.

After the last war it was decided to realign the western part of London Wall in order to provide a fast link between Moorgate and Aldersgate Street. The new dual carriageway is shown here before and after completion, and it may soon be extended westwards. Not all the surrounding architecture is of recent origin; parts of the ancient wall (which may once have been twenty-five feet high), can still be found amid the glass and concrete jungle. There is a good example to be seen in St. Alphage Garden.

33. FINSBURY CIRCUS, 1913

This is the north-east arc of Finsbury Circus; it could easily be Bloomsbury for it is not the townscape that we are accustomed to in the City.

This area was once a great marsh just outside the city wall. In 1631 it was described as 'a rotten morish ground . . . with deep stinking ditches'. From 1675 to 1814, when the circus was laid out, it was the site of the Bedlam Lunatic Asylum — a popular place for Sunday afternoon strolls as the grounds were open to the public.

The circus was conceived as a means of improving the status of the area, and the residences were designed to attract wealthy City businessmen, but it was not very long before the houses were converted into offices. As land values have risen, so the original buildings have been replaced by much higher, grandiose structures which have unfortunately destroyed the proportions of this interesting piece of late Georgian town planning.

34. BROAD STREET STATION, c1890

Broad Street Station used to be one of
London's busiest termini, but today it receives
only a thin trickle of traffic. The building,
which was put up in 1865, must once have
looked very handsome with its white Suffolk
bricks, red terracotta and polished granite
pillars; now it is just a uniform grey all over.
The iron canopy in front was replaced by a
stone building in 1913. Liverpool Street
Station, in the background, is usually teeming
with people. Plans have recently been put
forward for demolishing most of it and
rebuilding from scratch.

In the old view we catch a glimpse of some
Victorian horse-drawn omnibuses, which
according to contemporary accounts were
exceedingly draughty and uncomfortable. In
winter, straw was put down on the floor for
warmth, but worse still, the railings around
the top were rather low, and a sudden lurch
could almost send one over the edge!

35. HOUNDSDITCH, 1941

The camera is here pointing westwards along Houndsditch. The photograph shows damage caused by incendiary bombs. In the distance is the church of St. Botolph without Bishopsgate, its name signifying that it once stood just outside the City gate.

Houndsditch marks the line of the great ditch, dug during the reign of King John, which used to run along the outside of the city wall. It probably received its name either from the dead dogs that were often deposited there, or from the live hounds that were kept in the bottom of the ditch in readiness for City hunts. Following the Reformation, Houndsditch acquired a reputation for second-hand clothes dealers which it has retained right up to the present century. In the Plague of 1665 this area suffered more than any other part of London; during one fortnight over one thousand bodies were thrown into a local mass grave.

36. ST. ETHELBURGA'S CHURCH, c1905

This charming little church in Bishopsgate is hemmed in on both sides by shops and is easily missed by sightseers. Not only is it the City's smallest church, but it is also one of the oldest buildings in London, and was one of the few churches to escape the Fire of 1666. Henry Hudson received communion here in 1607 before setting sail for the frozen north where he discovered Hudson's Bay.

It is thought that the small shops in front originated as booths in the early sixteenth century. In 1905 they were occupied by an optician. There was fierce controversy when it was proposed to pull them down in order to widen the pavement, but the preservationists were eventually defeated in 1931. The front of the church was later restored, the plaster being removed and the stonework repaired. The beautiful west window is now clearly visible.

37. POULTRY, 1897

It's Queen Victoria's Diamond Jubilee, and the photograph captures all the pomp of that hot summer day when the Empire was at its zenith. Every nook and cranny has been decorated, and every balcony and window is crammed with excited spectators. Indeed, there seem to be as many people on the rooftops as in the street! In the foreground, straining to catch a glimpse of the procession, are Bluecoat boys from Christ's Hospital.

There was once a poultry market in this street, although by 1600 the poulterers had already moved away to Gracechurch Street and Newgate Market. Later, Poultry became noted for its taverns, most of which were destroyed in the Fire and never rebuilt. In 1872 the Gresham Life Assurance Society (on the right) replaced the ancient church of St. Mildred the Virgin. The Victorian buildings on the north side of the street have now disappeared, but several remain on the south side.

38. THE BANK, 1900

On 7 May 1900, thousands turned out to
cheer the Naval Brigade, heroes of the siege of
Ladysmith, and some people even had to seek
refuge on the roof of the Royal Exchange. The
five o'clock rush seems relatively peaceful in
comparison with this! *The Times* reported
that 'nothing in our time, at home or abroad,
has beaten the reception which was given to
the sailors and Marines from H.M.S.
Powerful on their triumphal march through
London', and at Lloyd's, where the heroes
were entertained to tea, 'hundreds of
underwriters were boiling over with patriotic
enthusiasm'.

Even the very heart of the City has been
changing. The Bank of England was enlarged
between the wars, although Soane's famous
windowless outer wall was retained. The latest
addition to the scene is the new Stock
Exchange tower (completed in 1970), the
bottom of which is visible on the left of the
modern photograph.

39. CORNHILL, 1925

More congestion — this time at the junction of Leadenhall Street, Cornhill and Gracechurch Street. The trouble seems to be roadworks in Cornhill, on the far side of the crossroads. There were no traffic lights here in 1925, just a sign exhorting you to 'drive slowly'. The corner has an interesting history. There was once a water-standard here with four spouts; it was such an important object that distances were measured to it from all parts of England, and in the nineteenth century one could still find wayside stones that indicated the number of miles from 'the Standard in Cornhill'.

The cornmarket from which Cornhill takes its name disappeared long ago. Today the street is the usual mixture of banks and insurance offices. An office block — to be occupied by a Belgian bank — will shortly be going up on the vacant site to the right of the photograph.

40. LOMBARD STREET, 1903

The Wright brothers were about to make
their first flight when this photograph was
taken. Now we are in the age of moon rockets,
yet Lombard Street retains the same quiet
dignity that it possessed in Edwardian times.
Closer inspection reveals that the buildings
have changed since then, but the architectural
styles have been carefully chosen to preserve
the personality of the street. You can still see
replicas of the richly decorated iron signs
which were so common in the City before the
mid-eighteenth century.

This famous thoroughfare is where the
Lombard money-lenders settled in the
12th century. Many years later the street was
inhabited by 'goldsmiths, bankers, merchants
and other eminent tradesmen', and even
today there is an almost continuous line of
banks on both sides of the road. Despite all
the changes in the City, there are some
remarkable examples of continuity.

41. ST. SWITHIN'S LANE, 1915

In 1915 London was no longer as confident as it had been at the time of the Diamond Jubilee. People had generally expected the war to be over by Christmas 1914, but now it looked as if it would drag on for several years to come.

On the corner of St. Swithin's Lane and Lombard Street a news-vendor displays the latest grim headlines from the Front, and every inch of advertising space has been taken up by recruiting posters: 'Go! It's your duty lad' . . . 'We're both needed to serve the Guns!' . . . 'It's our Flag — fight for it, work for it!' A large arrow points the way to the nearest recruiting office.

Notice in this photograph the fascinating steam-operated crane on the building site, and the contrast between 19th- and 20th-century modes of transport. Mansion House Place (now hidden by a Japanese bank) was known as George Street in 1915.

42. KING WILLIAM STREET, c1890

When the new London Bridge was built
between 1824 and 1831, it was only logical to
improve the approaches to it, for otherwise
the object of easing the flow of traffic would
have been defeated. Originally it was intended
merely to widen the approach to old London
Bridge, and divert traffic from the new bridge
into Fish Street Hill. But this would have
caused intolerable congestion, so a new road
(later named King William Street) was
sanctioned by Parliament in 1829.

Judging by the shadows, the old
photograph must have been taken on a hot
summer day round about noon. The road
looks very dusty, and no one seems in any
particular hurry to get anywhere. However, it
would be wrong to assume that the pace of life
in Victorian London was always this leisurely,
just as it would be wrong to assume that the
modern photograph shows typical traffic
conditions.

43. KING WILLIAM STREET, 1902

The statue of King William IV which once stood in King William Street is now situated at Greenwich. It was executed by a Mr. Nixon — a perfectionist who made two full-size models (one in Portland Stone) before producing the final version in granite. Just over fifteen feet high, and weighing twenty tons, it was unveiled in 1844. It had to be supported when the Metropolitan Railway was being dug beneath. The pedestal is actually round, but here it is shown draped in decorations for Edward VII's coronation.

The buildings that now surround this important intersection are twice the height of their Victorian predecessors, and make the street appear much more narrow and confined. The sedate hansom cab, complete with nosebag and trail of horse dung, has long since been replaced by the motor taxi with its trail of black skid marks!

44. UPPER THAMES STREET, 1910

There is little to be seen of Edwardian Upper Thames Street today. The warehouses belonging to the Apostle's Bread Company have vanished without trace, and Red Bull Yard now lies buried beneath Mondial House. In addition, the road has been widened and straightened, and the kerb posts removed.

The posts shown here are particularly interesting as a few proved to be old cannon. The base of one of them was uncovered, revealing the trunnions which fixed the barrel to the gun carriage. Although the City was once replete with cannon-shaped kerb posts, nearly all of them were fakes, and few, if any, had been used in war. The purpose of kerb posts was to protect pedestrians from encroaching vehicles, but they also served to assist drivers in negotiating awkward corners; the cart wheel would be turned against the post and not against the corner of some unfortunate building.

45. CANNON STREET STATION, 1958

In Victorian times the land immediately to
the east of Cannon Street Station was
occupied by the City of London Brewery, a
mass of warehouses, and the church of
Allhallows the Great. The brewery was
replaced by Red Bull Wharf (shown here) in
1901. After the last war the land that was left
derelict made an ideal car park, and the
vehicles have now been provided with shelter.

Today the whole area is dominated by the
new telecommunications centre, Mondial
House. The strong personality of this building
has provoked much comment. It is possible
that one hundred years from now it will be
preserved as an 'historic monument', just as
the black shell of the station is preserved
today. The paddle-steamer is a reminder of
the days when the river echoed to the faint
thud of paddle wheels battling with the tide.

46. LONDON BRIDGE, 1913

The most famous London Bridge of all was undoubtedly that built between 1176 and 1209 by Peter of Colechurch. It stood just to the east of the present one, complete with its drawbridge, chapel, houses, cornmills and waterworks. Its successor, Rennie's granite bridge, was opened in 1831; it lasted until 1967 when it was shipped off to Arizona. Rennie's bridge had never really been a success because even after widening in 1903–4 it simply wasn't broad enough for the traffic it was required to carry. The new pre-stressed concrete bridge, opened in 1973, is less than half the weight of Rennie's and forty feet wider. Notice the interesting contrast in the lighting provided on the old and new bridges, and the changing skyline on the south bank. A putting green was laid out on the roof of Adelaide House (on the left), which replaced the former Adelaide Buildings in 1924.

47. LONDON BRIDGE, east side, c1890

Just as the streets of late Victorian London were usually choked with horse-drawn traffic, so the Thames was clogged with shipping of all kinds — sailing barges, paddle-steamers, lighters, rowing boats — the forest of masts and funnels practically obscured London Bridge.

Today the river is nowhere near as busy; all that one is likely to see is the occasional string of barges, a police launch or a hydrofoil. Ships are now much bigger and often need the specialized loading facilities that are provided further downstream. Also, much river traffic has been killed off by road and rail transport.

On the right of the old photo, adjacent to the bridge, is the London Bridge Wharf where passengers used to embark for the popular Victorian resorts of Sheerness, Gravesend, Margate and Calais. By 1890 the service was less frequent than it had been in mid-century, but the arrival or departure of a boat always attracted a great crowd of spectators.

48. ST. DUNSTAN IN THE EAST, c1890

Before its destruction in the Great Fire, St. Dunstan's was a famous landmark. It had a tall, lead steeple that was visible from a great distance. The church was subsequently restored, and Wren added a new spire, but the main body of the church had to be rebuilt in 1818. St. Dunstan's was bombed during the war, but this time it was decided not to rebuild again. Instead, a public garden was laid out within the ruins by the Worshipful Company of Gardeners, and we now have flowers and a fountain in place of pews and a pulpit. The spire is still standing, and the garden (which won a Civic Trust Award) is a delightful spot to spend the lunch hour.

St. Mary's Aldermanbury has undergone similar treatment. In this case the remains of the church were transported to America and re-erected in Fulton, Missouri as a memorial to Sir Winston Churchill.

49. THE TOWER, *c*1900

In the old photograph the horizon is broken
only by the Monument, St. Paul's and an
occasional steeple. Now it is punctuated
everywhere by cranes and modern office
towers like the Kleinwort Benson building.

The Thames riverbank, too, has been
changing. Notice for instance how the trees in
the foreground have grown. Many centuries
ago the Thames was much wider and
shallower than it is now, and the bank was
further inland — probably along the line of
Lower Thames Street. When workmen were
digging the foundations of the present
Custom House (on the extreme left of the old
photo), they came across layers of mussel
shells and rushes, and between the road and
the river three lines of wooden embankments
were found. Similar ancient embankments
are now being uncovered at the Trig Lane site
near Blackfriars.

One building that doesn't seem to change is
the Tower, although nowadays it is full of
tourists, not prisoners!

50. TOWER BRIDGE, c1893

The finishing touches are here being put to Tower Bridge, four years later than expected. Today it is probably the most well-known bridge in the world. This particular design was only selected after much deliberation, and London might well have been graced with one of the many other schemes that were submitted; these included a high-level suspension bridge, approached by spiral ramps resembling the Leaning Tower of Pisa, and a proposal for a structure where a short length of road moved across the river on rollers mounted in piers. Once considered a miracle of hydraulic engineering, the machinery of Tower Bridge has now been electrified, and the bascules rarely open because so few large ships now venture this far up the river. The footpath high above the road had to be closed because too many people insisted upon jumping off it.

51. ST. MARY AXE, 1891

At the corner of Leadenhall Street and St. Mary Axe (now a one-way street) is a most intriguing church. St. Andrew Undershaft takes its name from a maypole, or shaft, which was set up outside the church every May Day throughout the 15th century. This custom died out in 1517 and the shaft was destroyed in 1549.

The buildings in Leadenhall Street in front of the church were about to be pulled down when the old photo was taken. One of them was occupied by a firm of 'electrical, marine, hot water, sanitary and general engineers', and in their window they advertised a 'patent system of lightning conductors, patronized by the Queen'. On the opposite corner was a varnish manufacturer. Now there is a bank on the former site, and opposite is the impressive glass wall of the Commercial Union Head Office, 387 feet high. The steelwork of this building was erected in only twenty-four weeks.

52. ALDGATE HIGH STREET, *c*1875

We are now on the very eastern edge of the
City, looking west. The City boundary is
marked by the stone obelisk on the corner of
Mansell Street. The City wall and the gateway
which gave the street its name were, until
1761, situated just off the photo on the right.
The Corporation did not welcome trams in
the City, so the line from Stratford, which was
opened in 1870, terminated here opposite the
Hoop and Grapes. This is incidentally
reputed to be the oldest licensed house in the
City.

A century ago the south side of the High
Street consisted mainly of butchers' shops,
and was generally referred to as 'Butcher
Row'. A few of these old buildings have
managed to survive virtually intact, and one
hopes that they will be preserved for a long
time to come.

Memory Lane

1. The City of London has long been famous for its pomp and circumstance, and perhaps the grandest spectacle of all was the occasion of Queen Victoria's Diamond Jubilee on 22 June 1897. The procession, which included representatives of most of the royal families of Europe, started out from Buckingham Palace and proceeded to St. Paul's and the Mansion House. From there it made its way to London Bridge (depicted here), returning to the Palace via Borough Road and Westminster Bridge.

2. This photograph was taken on the same day as no. 6 — 28 July 1871, looking in the opposite direction. Shoe Lane was being widened at the time. On the right, behind the hoarding, is the old Farringdon Market which was famous for its watercress. The lady behind the barrow appears to be doing a brisk trade selling apples and blackçurrants.

3. These Victorian tourists on a visit to the Tower of London seem more interested in the photographer than in the site of the scaffold!

4. Shoeblacks outside the Royal Exchange, *c*1900. In Victorian times streets were much dirtier than they are now, and crossing the road in wet weather often meant a thorough soaking in mud. Shoeblacks were thus always kept busy. They had their own trade societies; City shoeblacks wore red jackets while those in East London wore blue. The more conscientious members provided magazines and chairs for their customers.

5. Cloth Fair slums in 1877. It is easy to see why fires spread so quickly when houses were as flimsy and densely packed as this. These ancient and insanitary buildings were demolished shortly after the photo was taken when it was realised that they could not possibly be restored.

6. Paul Pindar Tavern at the corner of Bishopsgate and Half Moon Street, photographed on 8 September 1890, just prior to its demolition. The site is now covered by Liverpool Street Station. The tavern, which once formed part of the house of Sir Paul Pindar (erected c1600), can now be seen in the Victoria & Albert Museum.

7. The Oxford Arms Inn, Warwick Lane. This beautiful old galleried inn, only a stone's throw from St. Paul's, was pulled down in 1876. It was probably rebuilt after the Fire of 1666 on the same pattern as an earlier building.

8. The flogging box at Newgate Prison. This curious wooden construction was a combination of the pillory and the stocks. It was occasionally employed, up to the end of the nineteenth century 'to chastise the juvenile insolence of wicked boys'.

9. A London chimney sweep — indispensable in the days when everyone had a coal fire. 'One sees him everywhere', observed Mr. William Ryan in 1902, 'and the richness of his workaday complexion serves as well as an auditor's report to demonstrate his prosperity'.

10. Paviours ramming the road surface at the eastern end of the Holborn Viaduct on 14 September 1869. Today, of course, it would all be done by machinery.